COUNTRY
FARMHOUSE
KITCHEN

COUNTRY
FARMHOUSE
KITCHEN

TRADITIONAL HOME COOKING
AT ITS BEST

Consultant Editor: Judith Simons

Sebastian Kelly

This edition published in 1999 by Sebastian Kelly

© Anness Publishing Limited 1999

Produced by Anness Publishing Limited
Hermes House, 88–89 Blackfriars Road
London SE1 8HA

ISBN 1 84081 302 4

Publisher: Joanna Lorenz
Project Editors: Gaby Goldsack, Linda Doeser
Editor: Jenni Fleetwood
Designer: Siân Keogh, Axis Design
Illustrator: Anna Koska

Front cover: Lisa Tai, Designer; Thomas Odulate, Photographer;
Helen Trent, Stylist; Lucy McKelvie, Home Economist

Previously publiished as part of a larger compendium, *The Farmhouse Cookbook*

Printed in Hong Kong/China

1 3 5 7 9 10 8 6 4 2

The publishers would like to thank the following contributors: Carla Capalbo,
Jaqueline Clark, Maxine Clark, Frances Cleary, Carole Clements,
Stephanie Donaldson, Joanna Farrow, Christine France, Christine Ingram,
Judy Jackson, Patricia Lousada, Norma MacMillan, Katherine Richmond,
Laura Washburn, Steven Wheeler, Elizabeth Wolf-Cohen
They would also like to thank the following photographers: Karl Adamson,
Edward Allwright, James Duncan, John Freeman, Michelle Garrett,
Amanda Heywood, Patrick McLeavey

CONTENTS

INTRODUCTION 6

Soups & Appetizers 10

Vegetables 20

Egg & Cheese Dishes 34

Fish & Shellfish 42

Meat & Poultry 52

Desserts 74

Baking Goods 82

Preserves 90

INDEX 96

Introduction

Good cooking depends on the best-quality and freshest ingredients, so it is hardly surprising that some of the finest cooking in the world can be found in the traditional country farmhouse kitchen. Tomatoes still warm from the sun, carrots just pulled from the soil, freshly podded peas, and herbs plucked from the kitchen garden have a unique and special flavor, texture, and aroma. They taste best when cooked simply, without elaborate sauces and dressings that would smother their freshness and delicacy. Meals to satisfy the heartiest appetite are equally characteristic of the farmhouse kitchen. After all, a day spent plowing frost-hardened fields, a night spent lambing, or a sun-baked week of harvesting works up an appetite.

❧

Besides using home-grown vegetables and herbs, the farmhouse cook makes full use of the natural riches of the countryside. Nuts and mushrooms can be gathered in the woods, and sloes and rosehips can be picked from the hedgerows. Nothing is wasted. If there is an abundant fruit harvest, preserves and jellies will stock the pantry shelves, and chutneys and pickles are made from many different vegetables to spice up the winter months.

❧

The country cook makes the most of the fresh produce of each season and in this book you will find a mouthwatering collection of recipes inspired by the farmhouse kitchen— soups, pies, casseroles, stews, cakes, bread, and preserves. All are packed with flavor and will bring the taste of the country into any home.

Making Meat Stock

As every farmhouse cook will tell you, good homemade stock is the secret of successful meat soups, stews, casseroles, gravies and sauces.

INGREDIENTS

4–4½ pounds beef bones, such as shin, leg, neck and shoulder, or veal or lamb bones, cut into 2½-inch pieces
2 onions, unpeeled, quartered
2 carrots, roughly chopped
2 celery stalks, with leaves if possible, roughly chopped
2 tomatoes, coarsely chopped

4 quarts water
a handful of parsley stalks
a few fresh thyme sprigs or ¾ teaspoon dried thyme
2 bay leaves
10 black peppercorns, lightly crushed

Makes about 4 quarts

1

Preheat the oven to 450°F. Put the bones in a roasting pan or flameproof casserole and roast, turning occasionally, for 30 minutes or until they start to brown.

2

Add the vegetables and baste with the fat in the pan or casserole. Roast for another 20–30 minutes or until the bones are well browned. Stir and baste occasionally.

3

Transfer the bones and vegetables to a stockpot. Spoon off the fat from the roasting pan or casserole, add a little water and bring to a boil, scraping in any residue. Pour this liquid into the stockpot.

4

Add the remaining water. Bring just to a boil, skimming frequently to remove any foam. Add the herbs and peppercorns.

5

Partly cover the pot and simmer the stock for 4–6 hours, adding the liquid as necessary.

6

Strain the stock. Skim as much fat as possible from the surface. If possible, cool the stock and then chill it; the fat will set in a layer on the surface and can be removed easily.

Making Chicken Stock

Use turkey to make the stock, if you prefer.

INGREDIENTS

*2½–3 pounds chicken wings, backs
and necks
2 onions, unpeeled, quartered
4 quarts water
2 carrots, roughly chopped
2 celery stalks, with leaves if possible,
roughly chopped
a small handful of fresh parsley
a few fresh thyme sprigs or ¾ teaspoon
dried thyme
1 or 2 bay leaves
10 black peppercorns, lightly crushed*

Makes about 2½ quarts

1

Put the chicken pieces and the onions in a
stockpot. Cook over medium heat, stirring
occasionally, until lightly browned. Stir in
the water. Bring to a boil. Skim the surface.

2

Add the remaining ingredients. Simmer for
3 hours. Strain, cool and chill. When cold,
remove the fat from the surface.

Making Vegetable Stock

Vary the ingredients for this fresh-flavored stock according to what you have on hand.

INGREDIENTS

*2 large onions, coarsely chopped
2 leeks, sliced
3 garlic cloves, crushed
3 carrots, coarsely chopped
4 celery stalks, coarsely chopped
1 large strip of pared lemon rind
a handful of parsley stalks
a few fresh thyme sprigs
2 bay leaves
3½ quarts water*

Makes 3½ quarts

1

Put the vegetables, lemon rind, herbs and
water in a stockpot and bring to a boil.
Skim the surface.

2

Reduce the heat and simmer, uncovered, for
30 minutes. Strain the stock and let cool.

SOUPS &
APPETIZERS

~

Farmhouse Onion Soup

Slow, careful cooking is the secret of this traditional onion soup.

INGREDIENTS

*2 tablespoons sunflower or olive oil, or
a mixture
2 tablespoons butter
4 large onions, chopped
4 cups beef stock
4 slices French bread
1½–2 ounces Gruyère or Cheddar
cheese, grated
salt and freshly ground black pepper*

Serves 4

1

Heat the oil and butter in a deep saucepan and fry the onions briskly for 3–4 minutes. Reduce the heat and cook gently for 45–60 minutes.

2

When the onions are a rich mahogany brown, add the beef stock and a little seasoning. Simmer, partially covered, for 30 minutes, then taste and adjust the seasoning.

3

Preheat the broiler and toast the French bread. Spoon the soup into four soup dishes that can safely be used under the broiler. Place a piece of bread in each. Sprinkle with the cheese and broil for a few minutes, until golden.

Country Vegetable Soup

This satisfying soup captures all the flavors of the countryside. The basil and garlic purée gives it extra color and a wonderful aroma—so don't omit it.

INGREDIENTS

1½ cups fresh shelled fava beans, or
¾ cup dried great northern beans,
soaked overnight in water to cover
½ teaspoon dried herbes de Provence
2 garlic cloves, finely chopped
1 tablespoon olive oil
1 onion, finely chopped
2 small leeks, finely sliced
1 celery stalk, finely sliced
2 carrots, finely diced
2 small potatoes, peeled and finely
diced
4 ounces green beans
5 cups water
1 cup peas, fresh or frozen
2 small zucchini, finely chopped
3 tomatoes, skinned, seeded and finely
chopped
a handful of spinach leaves, cut into
thin ribbons
salt and freshly ground black pepper
fresh basil sprigs, to garnish

For the garlic purée
1 or 2 garlic cloves, finely chopped
½ cup basil leaves
¼ cup grated Parmesan cheese
¼ cup extra virgin olive oil

Serves 6–8

NOTE
To serve the soup, season and swirl a
spoonful of purée into each bowl and
garnish with basil.

1

To make the purée, process the garlic, basil
and Parmesan until smooth. With the
machine running, slowly add the olive oil
through the feed-tube. Alternatively, put
the garlic, basil and cheese in a mortar.
Pound with a pestle, then stir in the oil.

3

Heat the oil in a saucepan. Fry the onion
and leeks for 5 minutes, stirring
occasionally.

5

Add the potatoes, green beans and water.
Bring to a boil, then cover and simmer
for 10 minutes.

2

If using dried beans, boil vigorously for
10 minutes and drain. Place them or the fresh
beans in a saucepan with the herbs and
1 chopped garlic clove. Add water to cover by
1 inch. Bring to a boil and simmer for
10 minutes for fresh beans or about 1 hour for
dried beans. Set aside.

4

Add the celery and carrots, with the
remaining garlic clove. Cook for 10 minutes.

6

Add the peas, zucchini and tomatoes, with
the reserved beans. Simmer for
25–30 minutes. Add the spinach, season to
taste, and simmer for 5 minutes.

Summer Tomato Soup

The success of this soup depends on using ripe, full-flavored tomatoes, such as the oval plum variety. It is traditionally made when the tomato season is at its peak.

INGREDIENTS

1 tablespoon olive oil
1 large onion, chopped
1 carrot, chopped
2¼ pounds ripe tomatoes, cored and quartered
2 garlic cloves, chopped
5 fresh thyme sprigs
4 or 5 fresh marjoram sprigs, plus extra for garnish
1 bay leaf
3 tablespoons sour cream or yogurt, plus a little extra to garnish
salt and freshly ground black pepper

Serves 4

1

Heat the olive oil in a large saucepan. Cook the onion and carrot over medium heat for 3–4 minutes, until just softened, stirring occasionally.

2

Add the tomatoes, garlic and herbs. Simmer, covered, for 30 minutes, then sieve the soup into a clean pan. Stir in the sour cream or yogurt and season. Reheat gently and serve garnished with cream or yogurt and marjoram.

Pumpkin Soup

When the first frosts of autumn chill the air, bright orange pumpkins are a vivid sight in gardens and at country markets. Pumpkin soup is delicious.

INGREDIENTS

2 tablespoons butter
1 large onion, chopped
2 shallots, chopped
2 potatoes, peeled and cubed
6 cups cubed pumpkin flesh
8 cups chicken or vegetable stock
½ teaspoon ground cumin
pinch of freshly grated nutmeg
salt and freshly ground black pepper
fresh parsley or chives, to garnish

Serves 6–8

1

Melt the butter in a large saucepan and cook the onion and shallots for 4–5 minutes, until just softened. Add the potatoes, pumpkin, stock and spices with a little salt and black pepper. Simmer, covered, for about 1 hour, stirring occasionally.

2

With a slotted spoon, transfer the cooked vegetables to a food processor. Process until smooth, adding a little of the cooking liquid if needed. Stir the purée into the cooking liquid remaining in the pan. Adjust the seasoning and reheat gently. Serve garnished with the fresh herbs.

Stuffed Garlic Mushrooms

Flavorful portobello mushrooms make a simply delicious appetizer when stuffed and baked.

INGREDIENTS

1 onion, chopped
6 tablespoons butter
8 portobello mushrooms of similar size
¼ cup wild or dried mushrooms, soaked
in warm water for 20 minutes
1 garlic clove, crushed
1½ cups fresh bread crumbs
1 egg
5 tablespoons chopped fresh parsley
1 tablespoon chopped fresh thyme
4 ounces prosciutto, thinly sliced
salt and freshly ground black pepper
fresh parsley, to garnish

Serves 4

1

Preheat the oven to 375°F. Fry the onions gently in half the butter until soft. Break off the stems of the portobello mushrooms, setting the caps aside. Drain the dried or wild mushrooms and chop these and the portobello mushroom stems finely. Add to the onion, with the garlic, and cook for 2–3 minutes more.

2

Put the mixture in a bowl and add the bread crumbs, egg, herbs and seasoning. Melt the remaining butter and brush it over the mushroom caps. Arrange them on a baking sheet and spoon in the filling. Bake for 20–30 minutes, until well browned. Top each mushroom with a strip of prosciutto, garnish with parsley and serve.

Mushroom Salad with Prosciutto

Ribbons of ham and pancake, tossed with wild mushrooms and salad greens,
provide a feast for the eyes and the palate.

INGREDIENTS

3 tablespoons butter
1 pound assorted wild and cultivated
mushrooms, sliced
¼ cup sherry
juice of ½ lemon
mixed lettuce greens
2 tablespoons walnut oil
6 ounces prosciutto, cut into ribbons

For the pancake ribbons
¼ cup all-purpose flour
5 tablespoons milk
1 egg
¼ cup grated Parmesan cheese
¼ cup chopped fresh herbs
salt and freshly ground black pepper

Serves 4

1

To make the pancakes, mix the flour and milk in a bowl. Beat in the egg, cheese, herbs and seasoning. Pour enough of the mixture into a hot, greased frying pan to coat the bottom of it. When set, turn the pancake over and cook briefly on the other side. Cool, then roll up and slice into ribbons. Repeat with the remaining batter.

2

Cook the mushrooms in the butter for 6–8 minutes. Add the sherry and lemon juice, and season to taste.

3

Toss the lettuce in the oil and arrange on plates. Place the prosciutto and pancake ribbons in the center and spoon on the mushrooms.

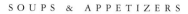

Country-style Pâté with Leeks

A rough pâté is very much a feature of the farmhouse kitchen. Cooked slowly so that all the flavors combine, then pressed, it makes a perfect appetizer or light lunch.

INGREDIENTS

1 tablespoon butter
1 pound leeks (white and pale green parts), sliced
2 or 3 large garlic cloves, finely chopped
2¼ pounds lean pork leg or shoulder, trimmed and cubed
5 ounces lean bacon strips
1½ teaspoons chopped fresh thyme
3 fresh sage leaves, finely chopped
¼ teaspoon quatre épices (mixed ground cloves, cinnamon, nutmeg and black pepper)
¼ teaspoon ground cumin
pinch of freshly grated nutmeg
½ teaspoon salt
1 teaspoon freshly ground black pepper
1 bay leaf

Serves 8–10

1

Melt the butter in a large, heavy saucepan, add the leeks, then cover and sweat over a low heat for 10 minutes, stirring occasionally. Add the garlic and continue cooking for about 10 minutes, until the leeks are very soft, then set aside to cool.

2

Pulse the meat cubes in batches in a food processor to chop it coarsely. Alternatively, pass the meat through the coarse blade of a mincer. Transfer the meat to a large mixing bowl and remove any white stringy bits. Reserve two of the bacon strips for garnishing, then chop or grind the remainder, and mix with the pork in the mixing bowl.

3

Preheat the oven to 350°F. Line the bottom and sides of a 6-cup terrine with waxed paper or parchment paper. Add the leek mixture, herbs and spices to the pork mixture, with the salt and pepper.

4

Spoon the mixture into the terrine, pressing it into the corners and compacting it. Tap firmly to settle the mixture and smooth the top. Arrange the bay leaf and bacon strips on top, then cover tightly with foil.

5

Place the terrine in a roasting pan and pour in boiling water to come halfway up the side. Bake for 1¼ hours. Drain off the water, then return the terrine to the roasting pan and place a baking sheet on top. Weight with two or three large cans or a foil-wrapped clean brick while the pâté cools. Chill overnight, before slicing.

VEGETABLES

~

Leeks in Egg and Lemon Sauce

*Tender young leeks, picked fresh from the vegetable garden, cooked and cooled
in a tart, creamy sauce, taste absolutely superb.*

INGREDIENTS

*1½ pounds baby leeks, trimmed, slit
and washed
1 tablespoon cornstarch
2 teaspoons sugar
2 egg yolks
juice of 1½ lemons
salt*

Serves 4

3

Whisk the egg yolks with the lemon
juice and stir gradually into the cooled
sauce. Cook over very low heat, stirring
constantly, until the sauce is fairly thick.
Immediately remove from the heat and
continue stirring for 1 minute. Taste and
add salt or sugar as necessary. Cool slightly.

4

Pour the sauce over the leeks. Cover and
chill for at least 2 hours before serving.

NOTE
Do not let the sauce overheat after adding
the egg yolks or it may curdle.

1

Lay the leeks flat in a large saucepan, cover
with water and add a little salt. Bring to a
boil, lower the heat, cover and simmer for
4–5 minutes, until just tender.

2

Lift out the leeks, drain well and arrange
in a shallow serving dish. Mix 1 cup
of the cooking liquid with the cornstarch
in a saucepan. Bring to a boil, stirring
constantly, then cook until the sauce
thickens slightly. Stir in the sugar.
Cool slightly.

Braised Red Cabbage

The combination of red wine vinegar and sugar gives this dish a sweet, yet tart, flavor. In France it is often served with game, but it is also delicious with pork, duck or cold meats.

INGREDIENTS

2 tablespoons vegetable oil
2 onions, thinly sliced
2 apples, peeled, cored and thinly sliced
1 head red cabbage (about 2 pounds), trimmed, cored, halved and thinly sliced
¼ cup red wine vinegar
1–2 tablespoons sugar
¼ teaspoon ground cloves
1–2 teaspoons mustard seeds
⅓ cup raisins or currants
about ½ cup red wine or water
1–2 tablespoons red currant jelly
salt and freshly ground black pepper

Serves 6–8

1

Heat the oil in a large stainless-steel saucepan over medium heat. Fry the onions for 7–10 minutes, until golden. Stir in the apples and cook, stirring, for 2–3 minutes, until they are just softened.

2

Add the cabbage, red wine vinegar, sugar, cloves, mustard seeds, raisins or currants, red wine or water and salt and pepper, stirring until well mixed. Bring to a boil, stirring occasionally.

3

Cover and cook over fairly low heat for 35–40 minutes, stirring occasionally, until the cabbage is tender and the liquid is just absorbed. Add a little more red wine or water if the pan boils dry before the cabbage is tender. Just before serving, stir in the red currant jelly to sweeten and glaze the cabbage.

Salsify and Spinach Casserole

The spinach in this recipe adds color and makes it go further. However, if you have plenty of salsify, plus the patience to peel it, increase the quantity and leave out the spinach.

INGREDIENTS

juice of 2 lemons
1 pound salsify
1 pound fresh spinach leaves, well rinsed
⅔ cup chicken or vegetable stock
1¼ cups light cream or half-and-half
salt and freshly ground black pepper

Serves 4

2

Meanwhile, cook the spinach in a large saucepan over medium heat for 2–3 minutes, shaking the pan occasionally, until the leaves have wilted. Place the stock, cream and seasoning in a small saucepan and heat through very gently, stirring.

3

Grease a baking dish generously with butter. Drain the salsify and spinach and arrange in layers in the prepared dish. Pour the stock and cream mixture over the vegetables and bake for about 1 hour, until the top is golden brown and bubbling.

1

Preheat the oven to 325°F. Add a quarter of the lemon juice to a large bowl of water. Trim and peel the salsify. Place each peeled root immediately in the lemon water, to prevent discoloration. Bring a saucepan of water to a boil. Add the remaining lemon juice. Cut the salsify into 2-inch lengths, add it to the pan and simmer for about 10 minutes, until just tender.

Rosemary Roast Potatoes

These unusual roast potatoes use far less fat than conventional ones, and because they still have their skins they have more flavor, too.

INGREDIENTS

2¼ pounds small red potatoes
2 teaspoons walnut or sunflower oil
2 tablespoons fresh rosemary leaves
salt and paprika

Serves 4

NOTE
This preparation is also delicious with tiny new potatoes, especially if you roast them with chunks of red onion.

1

Preheat the oven to 475°F. Scrub the potatoes. If they are large, cut them in half. Place in a pan of cold water and bring to a boil. Drain.

2

Drizzle the oil over the potatoes and shake the pan to coat them evenly.

3

Put the potatoes in a shallow roasting pan. Sprinkle with the rosemary, salt and paprika. Roast for 30–45 minutes. Serve hot.

Baked Zucchini in Tomato Sauce

Zucchini and tomatoes have a natural affinity. Use fresh tomatoes, cooked and puréed, instead of canned, if possible.

INGREDIENTS

1 teaspoon olive oil
3 large zucchini, thinly sliced
½ small red onion, finely chopped
1¼ cups puréed tomatoes
2 tablespoons chopped fresh thyme
garlic salt and freshly ground black pepper
fresh thyme sprigs, to garnish

Serves 4

1

Preheat the oven to 375°F. Brush a baking dish with olive oil. Arrange half the zucchini and onion in the dish.

2

Spoon half the tomatoes over the vegetables. Sprinkle with some of the fresh thyme, then season to taste with garlic salt and pepper. Repeat with the remaining ingredients. Cover the dish and bake for 40–45 minutes. Garnish with thyme sprigs and serve hot.

Spicy Fried Potatoes

Give fried potatoes a hint of heat by tossing them with spiced vinegar.
Sliced peppers add a splash of color.

INGREDIENTS

2 garlic cloves, sliced
½ teaspoon crushed chilies
½ teaspoon ground cumin
2 teaspoons paprika
2 tablespoons red or white wine
vinegar
1½ pounds small new potatoes
5 tablespoons olive oil
1 red or green bell pepper, seeded and
sliced
coarse sea salt, to serve (optional)

Serves 4

1

Mix the garlic, chilies and cumin in a
mortar. Crush with a pestle, then stir in the
paprika and wine vinegar.

2

Bring a saucepan of lightly salted water to
a boil and cook the potatoes, in their skins,
for about 15 minutes, until almost tender.
Drain, peel, if preferred, and cut into
chunks. Heat the oil in a large frying pan;
sauté the potatoes until golden.

3

Add the spiced garlic mixture to the
potatoes with the sliced pepper and
continue to cook, stirring, for 2 minutes.
Serve warm or at room temperature. Scatter
with coarse sea salt, if desired, to serve.

Turnip Greens with Parmesan and Garlic

Farmhouse cooks know how to turn everyday ingredients into treats. Here, turnip greens are flavored with onions, garlic and Parmesan cheese. They do not need long cooking, because the leaves are quite tender.

INGREDIENTS

3 tablespoons olive oil
2 garlic cloves, crushed
4 scallions, sliced
12 ounces turnip greens, thinly sliced, tough stalks removed
¼ cup water
⅔ cup grated Parmesan cheese
salt and freshly ground black pepper
shavings of Parmesan cheese, to garnish

Serves 4

1

Heat the olive oil in a large saucepan and stir-fry the garlic and scallions for 2 minutes. Add the turnip greens and stir-fry for 2–3 minutes, so that the greens are coated in oil. Add the water.

2

Bring to a boil, lower the heat, cover and simmer, stirring frequently, until the greens are tender. Bring the liquid to a boil again, allow the excess to evaporate, then stir in the Parmesan and seasoning. Serve at once with extra shavings of cheese.

Glazed Carrots with Cider

Cooking young carrots with the minimum of liquid brings out the best of their flavor, while the cider adds a pleasant sharpness.

INGREDIENTS

1 pound young carrots
2 tablespoons butter
1 tablespoon brown sugar
½ cup cider
¼ cup vegetable stock
1 teaspoon Dijon mustard
1 tablespoon finely chopped fresh parsley

Serves 4

NOTE
If the carrots are cooked before the liquid in the saucepan has reduced, transfer the carrots to a serving dish and rapidly boil the liquid until thick. Pour the liquid over the carrots and sprinkle with parsley.

1

Trim the tops and bottoms of the carrots. Peel or scrape them. Using a sharp knife, cut them into short thin sticks. Melt the butter in a frying pan and sauté the carrots for 4–5 minutes.

2

Sprinkle on the sugar and cook, stirring, for 1 minute. Add the cider and stock, bring to a boil and stir in the mustard. Partially cover the pan and simmer for 10–12 minutes, until the carrots are just tender. Remove the lid and continue cooking until the liquid has reduced to a thick sauce. Toss the carrots with the parsley and spoon into a warmed serving dish.

Carrot, Apple and Orange Coleslaw

This dish is as delicious as it is easy to make. The garlic and herb dressing adds the necessary contrast to the sweetness of the salad.

INGREDIENTS

12 ounces young carrots, finely grated
2 apples
1 tablespoon lemon juice
1 large orange, peeled and segmented

For the dressing
3 tablespoons olive oil
¼ cup sunflower oil
3 tablespoons lemon juice
1 garlic clove, crushed
¼ cup plain yogurt
1 tablespoon chopped mixed fresh herbs
salt and freshly ground black pepper

Serves 4

1

Place the carrots in a large serving bowl. Quarter the apples, remove the core from each wedge and then slice thinly. Sprinkle the apples with lemon juice to prevent discoloration, then add to the carrots, with the orange segments.

2

To make the dressing, place the oils, lemon juice and garlic in a jar with a tight-fitting lid and shake vigorously. Add the remaining ingredients and shake again. Just before serving, pour the dressing over the salad and toss well.

Brussels Sprouts with Chestnuts

A traditional Christmas speciality, this combination of crisp, tender Brussels sprouts and chestnuts is perennially popular.

INGREDIENTS

8 ounces chestnuts
½ cup milk
4 cups small tender Brussels sprouts, trimmed
2 tablespoons butter
1 shallot, finely chopped
2–3 tablespoons dry white wine or water

Serves 4–6

1

Cut a cross in the bottom of each chestnut. Bring a saucepan of water to a boil, drop in the chestnuts and boil for 6–8 minutes. Peel while still warm, then return to the clean pan. Add the milk and enough water to cover the chestnuts. Simmer for 12–15 minutes. Drain and set aside.

2

Remove any wilted or yellow leaves from the Brussels sprouts. Trim the root end but leave intact or the leaves will separate. Using a small knife, cut a cross in the bottom of each sprout.

3

Melt the butter in a large, heavy frying pan, and cook the shallot for 1–2 minutes, until just softened. Add the Brussels sprouts and wine or water. Cover and cook over medium heat for 6–8 minutes, shaking the pan occasionally and adding a little more water if necessary.

4

Add the poached chestnuts and toss gently, then cover and cook for 3–5 minutes more. Serve immediately.

Leek and Onion Tart

This unusual recipe isn't a normal tart with pastry, but an all-in-one savory slice that is excellent served as an accompaniment to roast meat.

INGREDIENTS

4 tbsp unsalted butter
12 oz leeks, sliced thinly
2 cups self-rising flour
½ cup Crisco
⅔ cup water
salt and freshly ground
black pepper

Serves 4

1

Preheat the oven to 400°F. Melt the butter
in a pan and sauté the leeks until soft.
Season well.

2

Mix the flour, fat and water together in a
bowl to make a soft but sticky dough.
Mix into the leek mixture in the pan. Place
in a greased shallow ovenproof dish and bake
for 30 minutes, or until brown and crispy.
Serve sliced, as a vegetable accompaniment.

Squash à la Greque

A traditional French-style dish that is usually made with mushrooms.
Make sure that you cook the baby squash until they are quite tender,
so they can fully absorb the delicious flavors of the marinade.

6 oz pattypan squash
1 cup white wine
juice of 2 lemons
fresh thyme sprig
bay leaf
small bunch of fresh chervil,
coarsely chopped
¼ tsp coriander seeds, crushed
¼ tsp black peppercorns, crushed
5 tbsp olive oil

Serves 4

1

Blanch the pattypan squash in boiling
water for 3 minutes, and then refresh them
in cold water.

2

Place all the remaining ingredients in a pan,
add ⅔ cup of water and simmer for 10
minutes, covered. Add the patty pans and
cook for 10 minutes. Remove with a slotted
spoon when they are cooked and tender
to the bite.

3

Reduce the liquid by boiling hard for
10 minutes. Strain it and pour it over the
squashes. Leave until cool for the flavors to
be absorbed. Serve cold.

Stuffed Parsleyed Onions

Although devised as a vegetarian dish, these stuffed onions make a wonderful accompaniment to meat dishes, or an appetizing supper dish with crusty bread and a salad.

INGREDIENTS

4 large onions
4 tablespoons cooked rice
4 teaspoons finely chopped fresh
parsley, plus extra to garnish
4 tablespoons finely grated
sharp Cheddar cheese
salt and pepper
2 tablespoons olive oil
1 tablespoon white wine, to moisten

Serves 4

1

Cut a slice from the top of each onion and scoop out the center to leave a thick shell.

2

Combine all the remaining ingredients, moistening with enough wine to mix well. Preheat the oven to 350°F.

3

Fill the onions and bake for 45 minutes. Serve garnished with parsley.

EGG & CHEESE
DISHES
~

Eggs in Pepper Nests

Pepper strips look pretty and provide an interesting nest for baked eggs topped with cream.

INGREDIENTS

2 red bell peppers
1 green bell pepper
2 tablespoons olive oil
1 large onion, finely sliced
2 garlic cloves, crushed
5–6 tomatoes, skinned and chopped
½ cup tomato juice
generous pinch of dried basil
4 eggs
8 teaspoons light cream or
half-and-half
pinch of cayenne pepper (optional)
salt and freshly ground black pepper

Serves 4

1

Preheat the oven to 350°F. Seed and thinly slice the bell peppers. Heat the olive oil in a large frying pan. Sauté the onion and garlic gently for about 5 minutes, stirring, until softened.

2

Add the bell peppers to the onion and sauté for 10 minutes. Stir in the tomatoes and juice, the basil and seasoning. Cook gently for 10 minutes more, until the peppers are soft.

3

Spoon the mixture into four ovenproof dishes. Make a well in the center of each and break in an egg. Spoon 2 teaspoons cream over the yolk of each egg and sprinkle with a little black pepper or cayenne. Bake for 12–15 minutes, until the white of the egg is lightly set. Serve immediately with crusty bread.

Cheese and Bacon Quiche

Quiches are great country fare, ideal for al fresco meals. To pack for a picnic, double wrap the pan in foil and support it in a sturdy box.

INGREDIENTS

*12 ounces unsweetened pastry, thawed
if frozen
1 tablespoon Dijon mustard
6 lean bacon strips, chopped
3 eggs
1½ cups light cream or half-and-half
1 onion, chopped
5 ounces Gruyère cheese, diced
salt and freshly ground black pepper
fresh parsley, to garnish*

Serves 6–8

1

Preheat the oven to 400°F. Roll out the pastry and line a 9-inch pie pan. Prick the bottom of the pastry shell and bake for 15 minutes. Brush the shell with mustard and bake for 5 minutes more. Reduce the oven temperature to 350°F.

2

Fry the bacon until crisp and browned. Beat the eggs and cream, season with salt and pepper and set aside.

3

Drain the bacon. Pour off most of the fat from the pan, add the onion and cook gently for about 15 minutes.

4

Sprinkle half the cheese over the pastry, then the onion, followed by the bacon and remaining cheese. Pour in the egg mixture and bake for 35–45 minutes, until set. Serve warm, garnished with parsley.

Eggs Baked in Ham and Potato Hash

INGREDIENTS

4 tablespoons (½ stick) butter
1 large onion, chopped
12 ounces cooked ham, diced
1 pound cooked potatoes, diced
1 cup grated Cheddar cheese
2 tablespoons ketchup
2 tablespoons Worcestershire sauce
6 eggs
few drops of Tabasco sauce
salt and freshly ground black pepper
chopped fresh parsley, to garnish

Serves 6

3

Make six wells in the hash. Break each egg in turn into a small bowl or saucer and slip into one of the wells.

4

Melt the remaining butter. Season with Tabasco sauce, then dribble the seasoned butter over the eggs and hash. Bake for 15–20 minutes or until the eggs are set. Garnish with parsley and serve.

1

Preheat the oven to 325°F. Melt half the butter in a frying pan. Cook the onion until soft, stirring occasionally, then place it in a bowl and stir in the ham, potatoes, cheese, ketchup and Worcestershire sauce.

2

Season the mixture and spread it in a buttered baking dish in a layer about 1 inch deep. Bake for 10 minutes.

Omelet with Herbs

Sometimes the simplest dishes are the most satisfying. Fresh farm eggs, sour cream and herbs make a speedy but superb meal.

INGREDIENTS

2 eggs
1 tablespoon butter
1 tablespoon crème fraîche or sour cream
1 teaspoon chopped fresh mixed herbs (such as tarragon, chives, parsley or marjoram)
salt and freshly ground black pepper

Serves 1

VARIATIONS

Other omelet fillings could include sautéed sliced mushrooms, diced ham or crumbled crisp bacon, creamed spinach or thick tomato sauce and grated cheese.

1

Beat the eggs and salt and pepper in a bowl. Melt the butter in an omelet pan until foamy, then pour in the eggs. When the mixture starts to set on the bottom of the pan, lift up the sides with a spatula and tilt the pan to allow the uncooked egg to run underneath.

2

When the omelet is set, but still soft on top, spoon the crème fraîche or sour cream over the center and sprinkle with the herbs. Hold the pan over a warmed plate. With a spatula, lift one edge of the omelet and fold it over the middle. Tilt the pan so that the omelet folds into thirds and slide it out onto the plate.

Egg-stuffed Tomatoes

Effective, but surprisingly easy to prepare, this is the perfect dish for a quick lunch. For the most enjoyable result, eat immediately.

INGREDIENTS

¾ cup mayonnaise
2 tablespoons snipped fresh chives
2 tablespoons torn fresh basil leaves
2 tablespoons chopped fresh parsley
4 ripe tomatoes
4 hard-cooked eggs, sliced
salt
lettuce leaves, to serve

Serves 4

1

Mix the mayonnaise and herbs in a small bowl and set aside. Place the tomatoes core-end down and make deep cuts to within ½-inch of the bottom. (There should be the same number of cuts in each tomato as there are slices of egg.)

2

Fan open the tomatoes and sprinkle with salt, then insert an egg slice into each slit. Place each stuffed tomato on a plate with lettuce leaves and serve with the herb mayonnaise.

Cauliflower with Cheese Sauce

This dish is equally good made with broccoli. Serve it with bacon for a special treat.

INGREDIENTS

*1 pound cauliflower, broken into
florets
3 tablespoons butter
6 tablespoons all-purpose flour
1½ cups milk
1 bay leaf
pinch of grated nutmeg
1 tablespoon Dijon mustard
1½ cups grated Gruyère or Emmenthal
cheese
salt and freshly ground black pepper*

Serves 4–6

1

Preheat the oven to 350°F. Lightly butter a
large gratin pan or shallow baking dish.

2

Bring a large saucepan of salted water to a
boil, add the cauliflower florets and cook
for 6–8 minutes, until just tender.

3

Melt the butter in a heavy saucepan over
medium heat, add the flour and cook until
just golden, stirring occasionally. Gradually
add the milk, stirring constantly until the
sauce boils and thickens. Add the bay leaf
and salt, pepper and nutmeg. Add the
mustard. Reduce the heat and simmer for
5 minutes, stirring occasionally, then
remove the bay leaf. Stir in half the cheese.

4

Arrange the cauliflower in the pan.
Pour the cheese sauce on top and sprinkle
with the remaining cheese. Bake for about
20 minutes, until bubbly and
well browned.

Poached Eggs with Spinach

When the vegetable garden yields fresh spinach, serve this simple dish.

INGREDIENTS

2 tablespoons butter
1 pound baby spinach leaves, well rinsed
½ teaspoon vinegar
4 eggs
salt and freshly ground black pepper

For the hollandaise sauce
2 egg yolks
1 tablespoon lemon juice
1 tablespoon water
12 tablespoons (1½ sticks) butter
salt and white pepper

Serves 4

NOTE
For a well-shaped poached egg, swirl the water whirlpool-fashion before slipping the egg into the center.

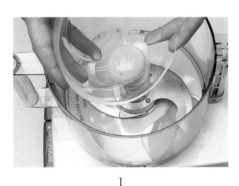

1

Make the hollandaise sauce. Mix the egg yolks, lemon juice and water in a food processor. Melt the butter in a small pan until foaming. With the machine running, slowly pour the hot butter into the processor in a thin stream. Season the thickened sauce with more lemon juice if needed and salt and pepper. Transfer the sauce to a bowl, cover and keep warm.

2

Melt the butter in a heavy frying pan over a medium heat. Add the spinach and cook until wilted, stirring occasionally. Season and keep warm.

3

Bring a pan of lightly salted water to a boil and add the vinegar. Break an egg into a saucer and slide the egg into the water. Reduce the heat and simmer for a few minutes until the white is set and the yolk is still soft. Remove with a slotted spoon and drain. Trim any untidy edges with scissors and keep the poached egg warm. Poach the remaining eggs in the same way.

4

To serve, spoon the spinach onto warmed plates and make a hollow in each mound. Place the eggs on top and pour a little hollandaise sauce on top.

FISH &
SHELLFISH

~

Chunky Seafood Stew

There's no more pleasant a way of spending an evening than sitting around the scrubbed farmhouse table and tucking into an excellent seafood stew.

INGREDIENTS

3 tablespoons olive oil
2 large onions, chopped
1 green bell pepper, seeded and sliced
3 carrots, chopped
3 garlic cloves, crushed
2 tablespoons tomato paste
2 cans (14 ounces each) chopped tomatoes
3 tablespoons chopped fresh parsley
1 teaspoon chopped fresh thyme
1 tablespoon shredded fresh basil leaves
½ cup dry white wine
1 pound shrimp, peeled and deveined, or cooked peeled shrimp
3–3½ pounds mussels or clams (in shells), or a mixture, thoroughly cleaned
2 pounds halibut or other firm, white fish fillets, cut into 2-inch chunks
1½ cups fish stock or water
salt and freshly ground black pepper
extra chopped fresh herbs, to garnish

Serves 6

2

Stir in the tomato paste, canned tomatoes, herbs and wine. Bring to a boil, lower the heat and simmer for 20 minutes. Add the shrimp, mussels and/or clams, fish pieces and stock or water. Season with salt and pepper to taste.

3

Bring back to a boil, then simmer for 5–6 minutes, until the shrimp turn pink, the fish flakes easily and the mussels and clams open. If using cooked shrimp, add them for the last 2 minutes only. Serve in large soup plates, garnished with chopped herbs.

1

Heat the oil in a flameproof casserole. Add the onions, green bell pepper, carrots and garlic and cook for about 5 minutes, until tender.

Cod, Basil and Tomato with a Potato Thatch

With a green salad, this makes an ideal dish for lunch or a family supper.

INGREDIENTS

2 pounds smoked cod
2½ cups white cod
5 cups milk
2 sprigs basil
1 sprig lemon thyme
10 tablespoons butter
1 onion, peeled and chopped
¾ cup flour
2 tablespoons tomato paste
2 tablespoons chopped basil
12 medium-size old potatoes
1⅓ cups milk
salt and pepper
1 tablespoon chopped parsley

Serves 8

1

Place both kinds of fish in a roasting pan with the milk, 5 cups water and herbs. Simmer for 3–4 minutes. Let cool in the liquid for about 20 minutes. Drain the fish, reserving the liquid for use in the sauce. Flake the fish, taking care to remove any skin and bone, which should be discarded.

2

Melt 6 tablespoons butter in a pan, add the onion and cook for about 4 minutes, until tender but not browned. Add the flour, tomato paste and half the basil. Gradually add the reserved fish stock, adding a little more milk if necessary to make a fairly thin sauce. Bring this to a boil, season with salt and pepper, and add the remaining basil. Add the fish carefully and stir gently. Transfer to an ovenproof dish.

3

Preheat the oven to 350°F. Boil the potatoes until tender. Add the remaining 4 tablespoons butter and the milk, and mash well. Add salt and pepper to taste and cover the fish, using a fork to create a pattern. If you like, you can freeze the pie at this stage. Bake for 30 minutes. Serve with chopped parsley.

Cod with Lentils and Leeks

This unusual dish is great for entertaining. The vegetables can be cooked ahead of time and the fish baked while the first course is served.

INGREDIENTS

1 cup green lentils, rinsed
1 bay leaf
1 garlic clove, finely chopped
grated zest of 1 orange
grated zest of 1 lemon
pinch of ground cumin
1 tablespoon butter
1 pound leeks, thinly sliced
1¼ cups whipping cream
1 tablespoon lemon juice, or to taste
1¼-pound thick cod or haddock fillet, skinned
salt and freshly ground black pepper

Serves 4

1

Put the lentils, bay leaf and garlic in a large saucepan and add enough water to cover by 1 inch. Bring to a boil, boil gently for 10 minutes, then reduce the heat and simmer for 15–30 minutes more, until the lentils are just tender.

2

Drain the lentils and discard the bay leaf, then stir in half the orange zest and all the lemon zest. Season with the ground cumin and salt and pepper. Transfer to a shallow baking dish or gratin dish. Preheat the oven to 375°F.

3

Melt the butter over medium heat in a saucepan, add the leeks and cook gently, stirring frequently, until just softened. Add 1 cup of the cream and the remaining orange zest and cook gently for 15–20 minutes, until the leeks have softened completely and the cream has thickened slightly. Stir in the lemon juice and season with salt and plenty of pepper.

4

Cut the fish into four pieces and remove any remaining bones. Season the fish with salt and pepper, place the pieces on top of the lentil mixture and press down slightly. Cover each piece of fish with a quarter of the leek mixture and divide the remaining ¼ cup cream among them. Bake for about 30 minutes, until the fish is cooked thoroughly and the topping is golden.

Trout with Almonds

This quick and easy recipe can be cooked for four, adapted by cooking the trout in two frying pans or in batches.

INGREDIENTS

2 trout, about 12 ounces each, cleaned
6 tablespoons all-purpose flour
4 tablespoons (½ stick) butter
¼ cup slivered or sliced almonds
2 tablespoons dry white wine
salt and freshly ground black pepper

Serves 2

NOTE

The easiest way to coat the trout is to put the flour in a large plastic bag and season with salt and pepper. Place the trout, one at a time, in the bag and shake until evenly coated. Shake off the excess flour from the fish.

1

Coat the trout in the flour, seasoned with salt and pepper. Melt half the butter in a large frying pan. When it is foamy, add the trout and cook for 6–7 minutes on each side, until the skin is golden brown and the flesh next to the bone is opaque. Transfer the fish to warmed plates and keep hot.

2

Add the remaining butter to the pan and cook the almonds until just lightly browned. Add the wine to the pan and boil for 1 minute, stirring constantly, until slightly syrupy. Pour or spoon over the fish and serve immediately.

Tuna with Garlic, Tomatoes and Herbs

In France, where this recipe originated, dried herbs are used, but fresh herbs are fine.

INGREDIENTS

4 tuna steaks, about 1 inch thick
(6–7 ounces each)
2–3 tablespoons olive oil
3 or 4 garlic cloves, finely chopped
¼ cup dry white wine
3 ripe tomatoes, skinned, seeded and chopped
1–2 tablespoons dried mixed herbs
salt and freshly ground black pepper
fresh basil leaves, to garnish

Serves 4

NOTE

Tuna is often served pink in the middle. If you prefer it cooked through, reduce the heat and cook for a few extra minutes.

1

Season the tuna steaks with salt and pepper. Set a heavy frying pan over high heat. When very hot, add the oil and swirl to coat. Add the tuna steaks and press down gently, then reduce the heat to medium and cook for 6–8 minutes, turning once, until just slightly pink in the center.

2

Transfer the steaks to a serving plate and keep hot. Add the garlic to the pan and fry for 15–20 seconds, then pour in the wine and boil until reduced by half. Add the tomatoes and herbs and cook for 2–3 minutes. Season with pepper and pour over the fish steaks. Serve, garnished with fresh basil leaves.

Pan-fried Garlic Sardines

Lightly fry a sliced clove of garlic to garnish the fish. This dish could also be made with small mackerel or fresh anchovies if available.

INGREDIENTS

8 fresh sardines
2 tablespoons olive oil
4 garlic cloves
finely grated rind of 2 lemons
2 tablespoons chopped fresh parsley
salt and freshly ground black pepper

For the tomato bread
2 large ripe beefsteak tomatoes
8 slices crusty bread, toasted

Serves 4

1

Gut and clean the sardines. Pat them dry with paper towels.

2

Heat the oil in a frying pan and cook the garlic cloves until soft.

3

Remove the garlic from the pan, then sauté the sardines for 4–5 minutes. Sprinkle with the lemon rind, parsley and seasoning.

4

Cut the tomatoes in half and rub them on the toast. Discard the skins. Serve each sardine on a slice of the tomato toast.

Broiled Sea Bass with Fennel

Fennel has an unmistakable flavor and goes particularly well with fish.

INGREDIENTS

1 sea bass, 4–4½ pounds, cleaned
4–6 tablespoons olive oil
2–3 teaspoons fennel seeds
*2 large fennel bulbs, with fronds
attached*
¼ cup Pernod
salt and freshly ground black pepper

Serves 6–8

1

With a sharp knife, make three or four deep cuts in both sides of the fish. Brush the fish with olive oil and season with salt and pepper. Sprinkle the fennel seeds in the stomach cavity and in the cuts. Set aside while you cook the fennel.

2

Preheat the broiler. Trim the fennel fronds and quarter the bulbs lengthwise. Remove the core and slice thinly. Reserve the fennel fronds. Put the fennel slices on the broiler rack and brush with oil. Broil for 4 minutes on each side, until tender. Transfer to a large dish or platter.

3

Place the fish on the oiled broiler pan and position about 5 inches from the heat. Broil for 10–12 minutes on each side, brushing occasionally with oil. Transfer the fish to the platter on top of the fennel. Garnish with the fennel fronds. Heat the Pernod in a small pan, light it and pour it, flaming, over the fish. Serve immediately.

Crab Cakes

These crab cakes are full of flavor thanks to mustard, horseradish and Worcestershire sauce.

INGREDIENTS

1 pound fresh lump crabmeat
1 egg, well beaten
1 teaspoon Dijon mustard
2 teaspoons prepared horseradish
2 teaspoons Worcestershire sauce
8 scallions, finely chopped
3 tablespoons chopped fresh parsley
1½ cups fresh bread crumbs
1 tablespoon whipping cream
(optional)
1 cup dry bread crumbs
3 tablespoons butter
salt and freshly ground black pepper
lemon wedges and fresh dill sprigs, for serving

Serves 3–6

1

In a mixing bowl, combine the crabmeat, egg, mustard, horseradish, Worcestershire sauce, scallions, parsley and fresh bread crumbs. Mix gently, leaving the pieces of crabmeat as large as possible. Season to taste. If the mixture is too dry to hold together, add the cream. Divide the crab mixture into six portions and shape into round, flat cakes.

2

Spread out the dry bread crumbs on a plate. Coat the crab cakes on both sides. Melt the butter in a frying pan. Fry the crab cakes for about 3 minutes on each side, or until golden. Add more fat if necessary. Serve with lemon wedges and dill.

Baked Stuffed Crab

Good cooking means meals that are good-looking as well as tasty. This recipe scores on both counts.

INGREDIENTS

4 freshly cooked crabs
1 celery stalk, diced
1 scallion, finely chopped
1 small fresh green chili, seeded and finely chopped
5 tablespoons mayonnaise
2 tablespoons fresh lemon juice
1 tablespoon snipped fresh chives
½ cup fresh bread crumbs
½ cup grated Cheddar cheese
2 tablespoons butter, melted
salt and freshly ground black pepper
fresh parsley sprigs, to garnish

Serves 4

2

Scrub the crab shells. Cut open the seam on the underside with scissors. The inner part of the shell should break off cleanly along the seam. Rinse the shells and dry them well.

1

Preheat the oven to 375°F. Remove the meat from the crab body and claws. Reserve the whole shells.

3

In a bowl, combine the crabmeat, celery, scallion, chili, mayonnaise, lemon juice and chives. Season and mix. In a separate bowl, toss together the bread crumbs, cheese and melted butter.

4

Pile the crab mixture into the shells. Sprinkle with the cheese mixture. Bake for about 20 minutes, until golden brown. Serve hot, garnished with parsley.

MEAT &
POULTRY

~

Pork Sausage and Puff Pastry Strudel

Country butchers sell a wonderful variety of sausages, including venison, pork and apple, and herb. All taste delicious when wrapped around a wild mushroom filling and baked in pastry.

INGREDIENTS

4 tablespoons (½ stick) butter
½ garlic clove, crushed
1 tablespoon chopped fresh thyme
1 pound assorted wild and cultivated mushrooms, sliced
1 cup fresh white bread crumbs
5 tablespoons chopped fresh parsley
12 ounces puff pastry
1½ pounds best-quality pork sausages
1 egg, beaten with a pinch of salt
salt and freshly ground black pepper

Serves 4

3

Make a series of slanting 1-inch cuts in the pastry on either side of the filling. Fold each end of the pastry over the filling, moisten the pastry with beaten egg and then cross the top with alternate strips of pastry from each side. Allow the pastry to rest for 40 minutes. Preheat the oven to 350°F. Brush the pastry with a little more egg and bake for 1 hour.

1

Melt the butter in a large frying pan and soften the garlic, thyme and mushrooms gently for 5–6 minutes. When the mushroom juices begin to run, increase the heat to boil off the liquid, then stir in the bread crumbs, parsley and seasoning.

2

Roll out the pastry on a floured surface to a 14 x 10-inch rectangle. Place on a large baking sheet. Skin the sausages. Place half of the sausage meat in a 5-inch strip along the center of the pastry. Cover with the mushroom mixture, then with the rest of the sausage.

Lamb Stew with Vegetables

*This farmhouse stew is made with lamb and a selection of young tender spring vegetables,
such as carrots, new potatoes, pearl onions, peas, green beans and turnips.*

INGREDIENTS

¼ cup vegetable oil
3–3½ pounds lamb shoulder, trimmed
and cut into 2-inch pieces
½ cup water
3–4 tablespoons all-purpose flour
4 cups lamb stock
1 large bouquet garni
3 garlic cloves, lightly crushed
3 ripe tomatoes, skinned, seeded and
chopped
1 teaspoon tomato paste
1½ pounds small potatoes, peeled or
scrubbed
12 baby carrots, scrubbed

4 ounces green beans, cut into
2-inch pieces
2 tablespoons butter
12–18 pearl onions or shallots, peeled
6 medium turnips, quartered
2 tablespoons sugar
¼ teaspoon dried thyme
1¼ cups peas
½ cup snow peas
salt and freshly ground pepper
3 tablespoons chopped fresh parsley or
cilantro, to garnish

Serves 6

1

Heat half the oil in a large, heavy frying
pan. Brown the lamb in batches, adding
more oil if needed, and transfer it to
a large, flameproof casserole. Add
3 tablespoons of the water to the pan and
boil for about 1 minute, stirring and
scraping the base of the pan, then pour the
liquid into the casserole.

2

Sprinkle the flour over the browned meat
in the casserole and set it over medium
heat. Cook for 3–5 minutes, until browned.
Stir in the stock, the bouquet garni, garlic,
tomatoes and tomato paste. Season with salt
and pepper.

3

Bring to a boil over high heat. Skim the
surface, reduce the heat and simmer,
stirring occasionally, for about 1 hour, until
the meat is tender. Cool the stew to room
temperature, cover and chill overnight.

4

About 1½ hours before serving, take the
casserole from the refrigerator, lift off the
solid fat and blot the surface with paper
towels to remove all traces of fat. Set the
casserole over medium heat and bring to a
simmer. Cook the potatoes in a pan of
boiling, salted water for 15–20 minutes,
then transfer to a bowl and add the carrots
to the same water. Cook for 4–5 minutes
and transfer to the same bowl. Add the
green beans and boil for 2–3 minutes.
Transfer to the bowl with the other
vegetables.

5

(Left) Melt the butter in a heavy frying pan
and add the onions and turnips with
another 3 tablespoons water. Cover and
cook for 4–5 minutes. Stir in the sugar and
thyme and cook until the vegetables are
shiny and caramelized. Transfer them to the
bowl of vegetables. Add the remaining
2 tablespoons water to the pan. Boil for
1 minute, incorporating the sediment, then
add this liquid to the lamb.

6

When the lamb and gravy are hot, add the
cooked vegetables to the stew and stir
gently to distribute. Stir in the peas and
snow peas and cook for 5 minutes, until
they turn a bright green, then stir in
2 tablespoons of the parsley or cilantro.
Pour the stew into a large, warmed serving
dish. Scatter the remaining parsley or
cilantro on top and serve.

Roast Leg of Lamb with Wild Mushroom Stuffing

Removing the thigh bone creates a cavity that can be filled with
a wild mushroom stuffing—the perfect treat for Sunday lunch.

INGREDIENTS

4–4½-pound leg of lamb, boned
salt and freshly ground black pepper
watercress, to garnish

For the wild mushroom stuffing
2 tablespoons butter, plus extra for
gravy
1 shallot or small onion, minced
8 ounces assorted wild and
cultivated mushrooms

½ garlic clove, crushed
1 fresh thyme sprig, chopped
1 ounce crustless white bread, diced
2 egg yolks

For the wild mushroom gravy
¼ cup red wine
1⅔ cups hot chicken stock
2 tablespoons dried cèpes, soaked in
boiling water for 20 minutes

4 teaspoons cornstarch
1 teaspoon Dijon mustard
1 tablespoon water
½ teaspoon wine vinegar
pat of butter

Serves 4

1

2

3

Preheat the oven to 400°F. To make
the stuffing, melt the butter in a large,
nonstick frying pan and gently fry the
shallot or onion without coloring. Add
the mushrooms, garlic and thyme. Stir
until the mushroom juices begin to run,
then increase the heat so that they
evaporate completely.

Transfer the mushrooms to a mixing bowl
and add the bread and egg yolks. Season
with salt and pepper and mix well. Allow
to cool slightly.

Season the inside of the lamb cavity, then
spoon in the stuffing. Tie up the end with
string and then tie around the joint so that
it does not lose its shape.

4

Place the lamb in a roasting pan. Roast
for 15 minutes per 1 pound for rare meat
and 20 minutes per 1 pound for medium-
rare. A 4-pound leg will take 1 hour and
20 minutes if cooked medium-rare.

5

6

Transfer the lamb to a warmed serving
plate. To make the gravy, spoon off all
excess fat from the roasting pan and brown
the sediment over medium heat. Add the
wine and stir in the chicken stock and the
mushrooms, with their soaking liquid.

Mix the cornstarch and mustard in a cup;
blend in the water. Stir into the stock
mixture to thicken it. Add the vinegar.
Season and stir in the butter. Garnish the
lamb with watercress and serve with the
wild mushroom gravy.

Lamb Pie with Pear, Ginger and Mint Sauce

Cooking lamb with fruit is an idea taken from traditional Persian cuisine.

INGREDIENTS

1 boned mid-loin of lamb, 2 pounds
after boning
salt and pepper
8 large sheets filo pastry
scant 2 tablespoons butter

For the stuffing
1 tablespoon butter
1 small onion, chopped
1 cup whole-wheat bread crumbs
grated rind of 1 lemon
6 ounces drained canned pears from a

14-ounce can (rest
of can, and juice, used for sauce)
¼ teaspoon ground ginger
salt and pepper
1 small egg, beaten
skewers, string and large needle to
make roll

For the sauce
rest of can of pears, including juice
2 teaspoons finely chopped fresh mint

Serves 6

1

Prepare the stuffing. Melt the butter in a pan and add the onion, cooking until soft. Preheat the oven to 350°F. Put the butter and onion in a mixing bowl and add the bread crumbs, lemon rind, pears and ginger. Season lightly and add enough beaten egg to bind.

2

Spread the loin out flat, fat side down, and season. Place the stuffing along the middle of the loin and roll carefully, holding it with skewers while you sew it together with string. Place in a large baking pan and brown the loin slowly on all sides. This will take 20–30 minutes. Let cool, and store in the refrigerator until needed.

3

Preheat the oven to 400°F. Take two sheets of filo pastry and brush with melted butter. Overlap by about 5 inches to make a square. Place the next two sheets on top and brush with butter. Continue until all the pastry has been used.

4

Place the roll of lamb diagonally across one corner of the pastry, without overlapping the sides. Fold the corner over the lamb, fold in the sides, and brush the pastry well with melted butter. Roll to the far corner of the sheet. Place, seam side down, on a buttered baking sheet and brush all over with the rest of the melted butter. Bake for about 30 minutes or until golden brown.

5

Blend the remaining pears with their juice and the mint, and serve with the lamb.

Country Meat Loaf

This dish makes a delicious alternative to a roast.

INGREDIENTS

2 tablespoons butter
1 small onion, finely chopped
2 garlic cloves, crushed
2 celery stalks, finely chopped
2 cups ground lean beef
2 cups ground pork
2 eggs
1 cup fresh white bread crumbs
3 tablespoons chopped fresh parsley
2 tablespoons snipped fresh basil
½ teaspoon fresh thyme leaves
½ teaspoon salt
½ teaspoon freshly ground black pepper
2 tablespoons Worcestershire sauce
¼ cup chili sauce or ketchup
6 lean bacon strips
fresh basil sprigs, to garnish

Serve 6

3

Use your hands to shape the meat mixture into an oval loaf. Carefully transfer it to a roasting pan.

4

Lay the bacon slices across the meat loaf. Bake for 1¼ hours, basting occasionally. Remove from the oven and drain off the fat. Place the meat loaf on a platter and let stand for 10 minutes before serving, garnished with basil.

1

Preheat the oven to 350°F. Melt the butter in a small frying pan. Cook the onion, garlic and celery over low heat for 8–10 minutes, until softened. Remove from the heat and let cool slightly.

2

In a large mixing bowl combine the onion, garlic and celery with all the other ingredients except the bacon and basil. Mix together lightly.

Sunday Best Beef Wellington

For a special occasion, nothing surpasses the succulent flavor of Beef Wellington. Traditionally, the beef is spread with goose liver pâté, but many country cooks prefer a pâté made from woodland mushrooms; use a variety with maximum flavor.

INGREDIENTS

1½ pounds fillet of beef, tied
1 tablespoons vegetable oil
12 ounces puff pastry
1 egg, beaten, to glaze
salt and freshly ground black pepper

For the parsley pancakes
½ cup all-purpose flour
⅔ cup milk
1 egg
2 tablespoons chopped fresh parsley

For the mushroom pâté
2 tablespoons butter
2 shallots or 1 small onion, chopped
4 cups assorted wild and cultivated mushrooms, chopped
1 cup fresh white bread crumbs
5 tablespoons heavy cream
2 egg yolks

Serves 4

1

Preheat the oven to 425°F. Season the fillet with several grindings of black pepper. Heat the oil in a roasting pan, add the beef and quickly sear to brown all sides. Transfer to the oven and roast for 15 minutes for rare, 20 minutes for medium-rare or 25 minutes for well-done meat. Set aside to cool. Reduce the oven temperature to 375°F.

2

To make the pancakes, beat the flour, a pinch of salt, half the milk, the egg and parsley together until smooth, then stir in the remaining milk. Heat a greased, nonstick pan and pour in enough batter to coat the bottom. When set, turn the pancake over and cook the other side briefly until lightly browned. Continue with the remaining batter—the recipe makes three or four pancakes.

3

To make the mushroom pâté, melt the butter in a frying pan and fry the shallots or onion for 7–10 minutes to soften without coloring. Add the mushrooms and cook until the juices run. Increase the heat so that the juices evaporate. Combine the bread crumbs, cream and egg yolks. Add the mushroom mixture and mix to a smooth paste. Let cool.

4

Roll out the pastry to a 14 x 12-inch rectangle. Place two pancakes on the pastry and spread with mushroom pâté. Place the beef on top and spread with any remaining pâté, then add the remaining pancakes. Cut out and reserve four squares from the corners of the pastry, then moisten the pastry with egg and wrap the meat. Decorate with the reserved pastry trimmings.

5

Put the Beef Wellington on a baking sheet and brush evenly with beaten egg. Bake for about 40 minutes, until golden brown. To ensure that the meat is heated through, test with a meat thermometer. It should read 125–130°F for rare, 135°F for medium-rare and 160°F for well-done meat.

Traditional Beef Stew and Dumplings

This dish can cook in the oven while you go for a wintery walk to work up an appetite.

INGREDIENTS

1 tbsp all-purpose flour
2½ lb stewing beef,
cubed
2 tbsp olive oil
2 large onions, sliced
1 lb carrots, sliced
½ pint / 1¼ cups Guinness
or dark beer
3 bay leaves
2 tsp brown sugar
3 fresh thyme sprigs
1 tsp cider vinegar
salt and freshly ground
black pepper

For the dumplings
½ cup chopped Crisco
2 cups self-rising
flour
2 tbsp chopped mixed
fresh herbs
about ⅔ cup water

Serves 6

1

Preheat the oven to 325°F. Season the flour
and sprinkle over the meat, tossing to coat.

2

Heat the oil in a large casserole and lightly
sauté the onions and carrots. Remove the
vegetables with a slotted spoon and
reserve them.

3

Brown the meat well in batches
in the casserole.

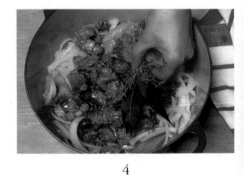

4

Return all the vegetables to the casserole and
add any leftover seasoned flour. Add the
Guinness or beer, bay leaves, sugar and
thyme. Bring the liquid to a boil and then
transfer to the oven.

5

After the meat has been cooking for 1 hour
and 40 minutes, make the dumplings. Mix
the Crisco and flour together. Add enough
water to make a soft, sticky dough.

6

Form the dough into small balls with floured
hands. Add the cider vinegar to the meat and
spoon the dumplings on top. Cook for a
further 20 minutes, until the dumplings
have cooked through and serve hot.

Steak and Kidney Pie, with Mustard and Bay Gravy

This is a sharpened-up, bay-flavored version of a traditional favorite. The fragrant mustard, bay and parsley perfectly complement the flavor of the beef.

INGREDIENTS

1 pound puff pastry
2½ tablespoons flour
salt and pepper
1½ pounds rump steak, cubed
6 ounces pig's or lamb's kidney
scant 2 tablespoons butter
1 medium onion, chopped
1 tablespoon English mustard
2 bay leaves
1 tablespoon chopped parsley
⅔ cup beef stock
1 egg, beaten

Serves 4

1

Roll out two-thirds of the pastry on a floured surface to about ⅛-inch thick. Line a 6-cup pie dish. Place a pie funnel in the middle.

2

Put the flour, salt and pepper in a bowl and toss the cubes of steak in the mixture. Remove all fat and skin from the kidneys, and slice thickly. Add to the steak cubes and toss well. Melt the butter in a pan and fry the chopped onion until soft, then add the mustard, bay leaves, parsley and stock and stir well.

3

Preheat the oven to 375°F. Place the steak and kidney in the pie and add the stock mixture. Roll out the remaining pastry to a thickness of ⅛ inch. Brush the edges of the pastry forming the lower half of the pie with beaten egg and cover with the second piece of pastry. Press the pieces of pastry together to seal the edges, then trim. Use the trimmings to decorate the top with a pattern of leaves.

4

Brush the whole pie with beaten egg and make a small hole over the top of the funnel. Bake for about 1 hour, until the pastry is golden brown.

Beef Casserole with Beans

This hearty casserole is slow-cooked to ensure that the meat is beautifully tender.

INGREDIENTS

*1¼ cups dried navy or lima beans,
soaked overnight in water
2–4 tablespoons oil
10 small onions, halved
2 carrots, diced
3–3½ pounds beef stew, cubed
6 small hard-cooked eggs in their
shells
1 teaspoon paprika
1 teaspoon tomato paste
2½ cups boiling water or beef stock
salt and freshly ground black pepper*

Serves 6–8

NOTE

If you have one, use a large slow cooker to cook the stew. You should not need to add extra liquid.

3

Stir the paprika and tomato paste into the oil left in the pan. Add a generous sprinkling of salt and pepper and cook for 1 minute. Stir in the boiling water or stock to incorporate the sediment, then pour the mixture over the meat and eggs.

4

Cover the casserole and cook for at least 8 hours, or until the meat is very tender, adding more liquid as needed. Take out the eggs, remove the shells and return the eggs to the casserole before serving.

1

Preheat the oven to 225°F. Drain the beans, place them in a saucepan and cover with fresh water. Bring to a boil. Cook rapidly for 10 minutes, skimming off the white froth and any bean skins that come to the surface. Drain.

2

Heat half the oil in a frying pan and sauté the onions for about 10 minutes, then transfer to a casserole with the carrots and beans. Heat the remaining oil and brown the beef in batches. Place it on top of the vegetables. Tuck the eggs between the pieces of meat.

Traditional Chicken Pot Pie

With its golden crust and rich chicken and vegetable filling, an old-fashioned chicken pot pie is a favorite family dish.

4 tablespoons (½ stick) butter
1 onion, chopped
3 carrots, diced
1 parsnip, diced
3 tablespoons all-purpose flour
1½ cups chicken stock
5 tablespoons medium sherry
5 tablespoons dry white wine
¾ cup whipping cream
¾ cup frozen peas, thawed
12 ounces cooked chicken meat, in chunks
1 teaspoon dried thyme

1 tablespoon finely chopped fresh parsley
salt and freshly ground black pepper
1 egg, beaten with 2 tablespoons milk, to glaze

For the pastry
1½ cups all-purpose flour
½ teaspoon salt
½ cup vegetable shortening
2–3 tablespoons ice water

Serves 6

1

For the pastry, sift the flour and salt into a mixing bowl. Rub in the shortening until the mixture resembles coarse bread crumbs, then add enough ice water to form a dough. Dust with flour, wrap and chill.

2

Preheat the oven to 400°F. Heat half the butter in a saucepan. Add the onion, carrots and parsnip and cook for 10 minutes, until softened. Remove from the pan with a slotted spoon.

3

Melt the remaining butter in the pan. Add the flour and cook for 2 minutes, stirring constantly. Stir in the stock, sherry and white wine. Bring the sauce to a boil and cook for 1 minute, stirring constantly.

4

Stir the cream, peas, chicken, thyme and parsley into the sauce. Season to taste with salt and pepper. Simmer for 1 minute, stirring, then transfer the mixture to an 8-cup pie dish.

5

On a lightly floured surface, roll out the pastry to a ½-inch thickness. Cover the pie and trim off the excess pastry. Dampen the rim of the dish. With a fork, press the pastry to the rim to seal. Cut decorative shapes from the pastry trimmings.

6

Brush the pastry all over with the egg glaze. Arrange the pastry shapes on top, then brush again with the egg glaze. Make one or two holes in the crust so steam can escape during baking. Bake the pie for about 35 minutes, until the pastry is golden brown. Serve hot.

Chicken and Corn Stew

Serve this rustic stew with biscuits; the combination works remarkably well.

INGREDIENTS

4 pounds chicken, cut into serving pieces
paprika
2 tablespoons olive oil
2 tablespoons butter
1 pound onions, chopped
1 green or yellow bell pepper, cored,
seeded and chopped
1 can (14 ounces) chopped tomatoes
1 cup white wine
2 cups chicken stock or water
3 tablespoons chopped fresh parsley
½ teaspoon Tabasco sauce
1 tablespoon Worcestershire sauce
2 cups corn kernels (fresh, frozen, or
drained canned)
1 cup fava beans (fresh or frozen)
3 tablespoons all-purpose flour
salt and freshly ground black pepper
Italian parsley sprigs, to garnish

Serves 6

1

Rinse the chicken pieces under cool water and pat dry with paper towels. Sprinkle each piece lightly with salt and paprika.

2

Heat the oil and butter in a large, heavy saucepan. Add the chicken pieces and fry until golden brown on all sides. Remove with tongs and set aside.

3

Reduce the heat to low and cook the onions and pepper for 8–10 minutes, until softened. Stir in the tomatoes, wine, stock or water, parsley and sauces. Turn up the heat and bring to a boil.

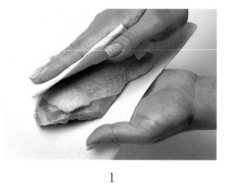

4

Return the chicken to the pan, pushing it down in the sauce. Cover, reduce the heat and simmer for 30 minutes, stirring occasionally.

5

Add the corn and beans and mix well. Partly cover and cook for 30 minutes more. Skim off or blot any surface fat.

6

Mix the flour with a little water to make a paste. Gradually add ¾ cup of the hot liquid from the pan. Stir this mixture into the stew and season with salt and pepper. Cook for 5–8 minutes more, stirring occasionally. Garnish and serve.

Chicken with Sloe Gin and Juniper

Juniper is used in the manufacture of gin, and this dish is flavored with both sloe gin and juniper. Sloe gin is easy to make and has a wonderful flavor, but it can also be bought ready-made.

INGREDIENTS

2 tablespoons butter
2 tablespoons sunflower oil
8 chicken breast fillets
12 ounces carrots, cooked
1 clove garlic, peeled and crushed
1 tablespoon finely chopped parsley
¼ cup chicken stock
¼ cup red wine
¼ cup sloe gin
1 teaspoon crushed juniper berries
salt and pepper
1 bunch basil, to garnish

Serves 8

1

Melt the butter with the oil in a pan, and sauté the chicken fillets until they are browned on all sides.

2

In a food processor, combine all the remaining ingredients except the basil, and blend to a smooth puree. If the mixture seems too thick, add a little more red wine or water until a thinner consistency is reached.

3

Put the chicken breasts in a pan, pour the sauce over the top and cook until the chicken is cooked through, which should take about 15 minutes. Adjust the seasoning and serve garnished with chopped fresh basil leaves.

Duck Stew with Olives

In this traditional method of preparing duck, the sweetness of the onions balances the saltiness of the olives.

INGREDIENTS

2 ducks, about 3¼ pounds each, quartered, or 8 duck leg quarters
1½ cups shallots, peeled
2 tablespoons all-purpose flour
1½ cups dry red wine
2 cups duck or chicken stock
1 bouquet garni
1 cup pitted green or black olives, or a combination
salt, if needed, and freshly ground black pepper

Serves 6–8

3

Stir in the wine, then add the duck pieces, stock and bouquet garni. Bring to a boil, then reduce the heat, cover and simmer for about 40 minutes, stirring occasionally.

4

Rinse the olives in several changes of cold water. If they are very salty, put them in a saucepan, cover with water and bring to a boil, then drain and rinse. Add the pitted olives to the casserole and continue cooking for 20 minutes more, until the duck is very tender.

5

Transfer the duck pieces, shallots and olives to a plate. Strain the cooking liquid, skim off all the fat and return the liquid to the pan. Boil to reduce by about one-third, then adjust the seasoning and return the duck, shallots and olives to the casserole. Simmer gently for a few minutes to heat through and serve.

1

Put the duck portions, skin side down, in a large frying pan. Cook over medium heat for 10–12 minutes, until well browned, then turn to color evenly. Cook in batches if necessary.

2

Pour 1 tablespoon of the duck fat into a large, flameproof casserole. Place the casserole over medium heat and cook the shallots until evenly browned, stirring frequently. Sprinkle with the flour and cook for 2 minutes more, stirring frequently.

Roast Turkey with Mushroom Stuffing

A fresh farm turkey tastes wonderful with a wild mushroom stuffing.
Serve it with a wild mushroom gravy for maximum impact.

10–12-pound free-range turkey
butter, for basting
watercress, to garnish

For the mushroom stuffing
4 tablespoons (½ stick) butter
1 onion, chopped
8 ounces wild mushrooms, chopped
1½ cups fresh white bread crumbs
4 ounces pork sausages, skinned
1 small fresh truffle, sliced (optional)
5 drops truffle oil (optional)
salt and freshly ground black pepper

For the gravy
5 tablespoons medium sherry
1⅔ cups chicken stock
4 teaspoons cornstarch
1 teaspoon Dijon mustard
2 teaspoons water
½ teaspoon red wine vinegar
pat of butter

Serves 6–8

1

Preheat the oven to 425°F. To make the stuffing, melt the butter in a saucepan and sauté the onion gently without coloring. Add the mushrooms and stir until their juices begin to flow. Transfer from the pan to a bowl and add all the remaining ingredients, including the truffle and truffle oil, if using. Season and stir well to combine.

2

Spoon the stuffing into the neck cavity of the turkey and enclose, fastening the skin on the underside with a skewer.

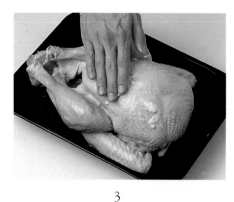

3

Rub the skin of the turkey with butter, place in a large roasting pan and roast for 50 minutes. Lower the temperature to 350°F and cook for 2½ hours more.

4

Transfer the turkey to a carving board, cover loosely with foil and keep hot. To make the gravy, spoon off the fat from the roasting juices, then place the pan over medium heat until the juices are reduced to a sediment. Stir in the sherry, then stir in the chicken stock.

5

Place the cornstarch and mustard in a small bowl. Stir in the water and wine vinegar. Stir this mixture into the juices in the roasting pan and simmer to thicken. Season and stir in a pat of butter. Garnish the turkey with watercress. Pour the gravy into a gravy boat and serve separately.

DESSERTS

~

Apple Mint and Pink Grapefruit Fool

Apple mint can easily run riot in the herb garden; this is an excellent way of using up an abundant crop.

INGREDIENTS

1 pound tart apples, peeled, cored and sliced
8 ounces pink grapefruit segments
3 tablespoons honey
2 tablespoons water
6 large sprigs apple mint, plus more to garnish
⅔ cup heavy cream
1⅓ cup custard

Serves 4–6

1

Place the apples, grapefruit, honey, water and apple mint in a pan, cover and simmer for 10 minutes, until soft. Leave in the pan to cool, then discard the apple mint. Purée the mixture in a food processor.

2

Whip the cream until it forms peaks and fold into the custard, keeping 2 tablespoons to decorate. Carefully fold the cream into the fruit mixture. Serve chilled and decorated with swirls of cream and sprigs of mint.

Summer Fruit Gâteau with Heartsease

No one can resist the appeal of little heartsease pansies. This cake would be lovely for a sentimental summer occasion in the garden.

INGREDIENTS

8 tablespoons margarine, plus more to grease mold
3¾ ounces sugar
2 teaspoons honey
1¼ cup self-rising flour
½ teaspoon baking powder
2 tablespoons milk
2 eggs, plus white of one more for crystallizing
1 tablespoon rose water
1 tablespoon Cointreau
16 heartsease flowers
superfine sugar, as required, to crystallize
confectioners' sugar, to decorate
1 pound strawberries
strawberry leaves, to decorate

1

Crystallize the heartsease pansies by painting them with lightly beaten egg white and sprinkling with superfine sugar. Let dry.

2

Preheat the oven to 375°F. Grease and lightly flour a ring mold.

3

In a large mixing bowl, mix the soft margarine, sugar, honey, flour, baking powder, milk and 2 eggs and beat well for 1 minute. Add the rose water and the Cointreau and mix well.

4

Pour the mixture into the pan and bake for 40 minutes. Let stand for a few minutes and then turn out onto the plate that you wish to serve it on.

5

Sift confectioners' sugar over the cake. Fill the center of the ring with strawberries. Decorate with crystallized heartsease flowers and some strawberry leaves.

Borage, Mint and Lemon Balm Sorbet

Borage has such a pretty flower head that it is worth growing just to make this recipe, and to float the flowers in summer drinks. The sorbet itself has a very refreshing, delicate taste, perfect for a hot afternoon.

INGREDIENTS

1 pound sugar
2 cups water
6 sprigs mint, plus more to decorate
6 lemon balm leaves
1 cup white wine
2 tablespoons lemon juice
borage sprigs, to decorate

Serves 6–8

1

Place the sugar and water in a saucepan with the washed herbs. Bring to a boil. Remove from the heat and add the wine. Cover and cool. Chill for several hours, then add the lemon juice. Freeze, and as soon as the mixture begins to freeze, stir briskly and replace in the freezer. Repeat every 15 minutes for at least 3 hours.

3

Place a small freezer-proof bowl inside each larger bowl and put inside a heavy weight, such as a metal weight from some scales. Fill with more cooled boiled water, float more herbs in this, and freeze.

2

To make the small ice bowls, pour about ½ inch cold, boiled water into small freezer-proof bowls about 2½ cups in capacity, and arrange some herbs in the water. Freeze, then add a little more water to cover the herbs.

4

To release the ice bowls, warm the inner bowl with a small amount of very hot water and twist it out. Warm the outer bowl by standing it in very hot water for a few seconds, then turn out the ice bowl. Spoon the sorbet into the ice bowls and decorate with sprigs of mint and borage.

French Apple Tart

For added flavor, scatter some slivered almonds over the top of this classic tart.

INGREDIENTS

For the pastry
*½ cup unsalted butter,
softened
4 tbsp vanilla sugar
1 egg
2 cups all-purpose flour*

For the filling
*4 tbsp unsalted butter
5 large tart apples, peeled, cored
and sliced
juice of ½ lemon
1¼ cups heavy cream
2 egg yolks
2 tbsp vanilla sugar
⅔ cup ground almonds,
toasted
2 tbsp slivered almonds, toasted,
to garnish*

Serves 8

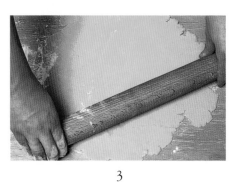

1

Place the butter and sugar in a food processor and process them well together. Add the egg and process to mix it in well.

2

Add the flour and process till you have a soft dough. Wrap the dough in plastic wrap and chill it for 30 minutes.

3

Roll the pastry out on a lightly floured surface to about 9–10 in diameter.

4

Line a pie pan with the pastry and chill it for a further 30 minutes. Preheat the oven to 425°F and place a baking sheet in the oven to heat up. Line the pastry case with wax paper and baking beans and bake blind on the baking sheet for 10 minutes. Then remove the beans and paper and cook for a further 5 minutes.

5

Turn the oven down to 375°F. To make the filling, melt the butter in a frying pan and lightly sauté the apples for 5–7 minutes. Sprinkle the apples with lemon juice.

6

Beat the cream and egg yolks with the sugar. Stir in the toasted ground almonds. Arrange the apple slices on top of the warm pastry and pour over the cream mixture. Bake for 25 minutes, or until the cream is just about set – it tastes better if the cream is still slightly runny in the center. Serve hot or cold, scattered with slivered almonds.

Spiced Red Fruit Compote

When summer fruits are at their best, what could be nicer than a simple compote?

INGREDIENTS

4 ripe red plums, halved
2 cups strawberries, halved
1¾ cups raspberries
2 tablespoons light brown sugar
2 tablespoons cold water
1 cinnamon stick
3 pieces of star anise
6 cloves
plain yogurt or fromage frais, to serve

Serves 4

1

Place all the ingredients, except the yogurt or fromage frais, in a heavy pan. Heat gently, without boiling, until the sugar dissolves and the fruit juices run.

2

Cover the pan and let the fruit infuse over very low heat for about 5 minutes. Remove the spices from the compote before serving warm with plain yogurt or fromage frais.

Rhubarb Cobbler

Typical English farmhouse fare: stewed rhubarb with biscuit topping.

INGREDIENTS

1½ pounds rhubarb, sliced
3 tablespoons orange juice
6 tablespoons granulated sugar
1¾ cups self-rising flour
1 cup plain yogurt
grated rind of 1 medium orange
2 tablespoons light-brown sugar
1 teaspoon ground ginger
plain yogurt or custard, to serve

Serves 4

1

Preheat the oven to 400°F. Cook the rhubarb, orange juice and ¼ cup of the granulated sugar over low heat. Transfer to an ovenproof dish.

2

To make the topping, mix the flour with the remaining granulated sugar, then gradually stir in enough of the yogurt to bind to a soft dough.

3

Roll out the dough on a floured surface to a 10-inch square. Combine the orange rind, brown sugar and ginger, then sprinkle over the dough.

4

Roll up the dough quite tightly, then cut into about ten slices. Arrange the dough slices over the rhubarb.

5

Bake the cobbler for 15–20 minutes, or until golden brown. Serve warm with plain yogurt.

BAKING
GOODS

~

Dark Fruitcake

With its colorful citrus and candied fruit topping, this tasty cake needs no further decoration.

INGREDIENTS

1 cup currants
1 cup raisins
⅔ cup golden raisins
¼ cup candied cherries, halved
3 tablespoons Madeira or sherry
12 tablespoons (1½ sticks) butter
1 cup dark brown sugar
2 extra large eggs
1¾ cups all-purpose flour
2 teaspoons baking powder
2 teaspoons each ground ginger,
allspice and cinnamon
1 tablespoon molasses
1 tablespoon milk
¼ cup candied fruit, chopped
1 cup walnuts or pecans, chopped

For the decoration
1 cup granulated sugar
½ cup water
1 lemon, thinly sliced
½ orange, thinly sliced
½ cup orange marmalade
candied cherries

Serves 12

1

Mix the currants, raisins, golden raisins and cherries in a bowl. Stir in the Madeira or sherry. Cover and leave overnight.

2

Preheat the oven to 300°F. Line and grease a 9-inch round springform pan. Cream the butter and sugar in a mixing bowl until light and fluffy. Beat in the eggs, one at a time.

3

Sift together the flour, baking powder and spices. Fold into the butter mixture in batches. Fold in the molasses, milk, dried fruit and liquid, candied fruit and nuts.

4

Spoon into the pan, spreading out so there is a slight well in the center of the mixture. Bake for 2½–3 hours, until a skewer inserted in the cake comes out clean. Cover with foil when the top is golden to prevent overbrowning. Cool in the pan on a rack.

5

To decorate, mix the sugar and water in a saucepan and bring to a boil. Add the citrus slices and cook for 20 minutes. Remove the fruit with a slotted spoon. Pour the remaining syrup over the cake and leave to cool. Melt the marmalade, then brush over the top of the cake. Decorate with the candied citrus fruit and cherries.

Cranberry Muffins

A tea or breakfast dish that is not too sweet.

INGREDIENTS

3 cups all-purpose flour
1 tsp baking powder
pinch of salt
½ cup superfine sugar
2 eggs
⅔ cup milk
4 tbsp corn oil
finely grated rind of 1 orange
5 oz cranberries

Makes 12

1

Preheat the oven to 375°F. Line a muffin pan with paper cases. Mix the flour, baking powder, salt and superfine sugar together.

2

Lightly beat the eggs with the milk and oil. Add them to the dry ingredients and blend to make a smooth batter. Stir in the orange rind and cranberries. Divide the mixture between the muffin cases and bake for 25 minutes until risen and golden. Let cool in the pan for a few minutes, and serve warm or cold.

Country Pancakes

Serve these hot with butter and maple syrup or jam.

INGREDIENTS

2 cups self-rising flour
4 tbsp superfine sugar
4 tbsp butter, melted
1 egg
1¼ cups milk
1 tbsp corn oil or
margarine

Makes 24

1

Mix the flour and sugar together. Add the melted butter and egg with two-thirds of the milk. Mix to a smooth batter – it should be thin enough to find its own level.

2

Heat a griddle or a heavy-based frying pan and wipe it with a little oil or margarine. When hot, drop spoonfuls of the mixture on to the hot griddle or pan. When bubbles come to the surface of the pancakes, flip them over to cook until golden on the other side. Keep the pancakes warm wrapped in a dish towel while cooking the rest of the mixture. Serve as soon as possible.

The Harvest Loaf

The centerpiece for celebrations when the harvest is safely gathered in, the harvest loaf is a potent symbol of country life. It is too salty to eat, but looks wonderful. Although there were many different designs of harvest loaf, the most enduringly popular was the wheatsheaf, symbolic as it is of the harvest and the vital importance of bread as "the staff of life."

INGREDIENTS

14 cups white bread flour
2 tablespoons salt
2 x ¼-ounce envelopes active dry yeast
3–3¾ cups lukewarm water
beaten eggs, to glaze

Makes two 1¾-pound loaves

1

Sift the flour and salt into a large mixing bowl and stir in the yeast. Add enough warm water to make a rough dough. Knead on a lightly floured surface for about 10 minutes, until smooth and elastic. Place the dough in a lightly oiled bowl, cover and let rise for 1–2 hours, until it has doubled in bulk.

2

Preheat the oven to 425°F. Oil and flour a large baking sheet. Roll out about 8 ounces of the dough into a 12-inch-long cylinder. Place it on the baking sheet and flatten slightly with your hand. This will form the body of the bread, symbolizing the long stalks of the wheatsheaf. The high salt content in the dough makes it easier to work, but the bread is more decorative than palatable.

3

Roll and shape about 12 ounces of the remaining dough into a crescent; place this at the top of the cylinder and flatten. Divide the remaining dough in half. Take one half and divide it in two again. Use one half to make the stalks of the wheat by rolling into narrow ropes and placing on the "stalk" of the sheaf. Use the other half to make a braid to decorate the finished loaf where the stalks meet the ears of

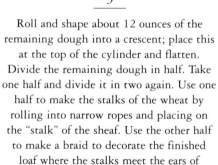

4

Use the remaining dough to make the ears of wheat. Roll it into small sausage shapes and snip each a few times with scissors to give the effect of the separate ears. Place these on the crescent shape, fanning out from the base until the wheatsheaf is complete. Position the braid between the stalks and the ears of wheat. Brush the wheatsheaf with the beaten egg. Bake for 20 minutes, then reduce the heat to 325°F and bake for 20 minutes more.

Potato Bread

Mashed potatoes make a lovely loaf. Make sure that the liquid is only warm, not hot, when added.

INGREDIENTS

*8 ounces potatoes, peeled and halved or
quartered
2 tablespoons vegetable oil
1 cup lukewarm milk
6 cups white bread flour
1 tablespoon salt
4 teaspoons active dry yeast*

Makes 2 loaves

1

Cook the potatoes in a saucepan of salted water for 20–30 minutes. Drain and reserve the cooking water. Return the potatoes to the pan and mash with oil and milk. Mix the flour, salt and yeast together. Put the potato mixture in a bowl. Stir in 1 cup of the potato cooking water, then gradually stir in the flour mixture to form a stiff dough.

2

Knead the dough for 10 minutes. Grease two 9 x 5-inch loaf pans. Roll the dough into 20 small balls. Place two rows of balls in each pan. Cover with plastic wrap and leave in a warm place to rise. Preheat the oven to 400°F. Bake the loaves for 10 minutes, then lower the heat to 375°F and bake for about 40 minutes more.

Irish Soda Bread

This traditional farmhouse loaf needs no rising, so it's perfect for unexpected guests.

INGREDIENTS

*2 cups all-purpose white flour, plus
extra for dusting
1 cup whole-wheat flour
1 teaspoon baking soda
1 teaspoon salt
2 tablespoons butter, softened
1¼ cups buttermilk*

Makes 1 loaf

1

Preheat the oven to 400°F. Grease a baking sheet. Sift the dry ingredients into a bowl. Make a well in the center and add the butter and buttermilk. Gradually incorporate the surrounding flour to make a soft dough. Gather the dough into a ball. Knead the dough on a floured surface for 3 minutes. Shape into a round.

2

Place the round on the baking sheet. Cut a cross in the top with a sharp knife. Dust with flour, then bake for 40–50 minutes, or until golden brown. Transfer to a rack to cool.

PRESERVES

~

Windfall Pear Chutney

The apparently unusable bullet-hard pears that litter the ground underneath old pear trees after high winds are ideal for this tasty chutney.

INGREDIENTS

1½ pounds pears, peeled and cored
3 onions, chopped
1 cup raisins
1 cooking apple, cored and chopped
⅓ cup preserved ginger
1 cup walnuts, chopped
1 garlic clove, chopped
grated zest and juice of 1 lemon
2½ cups cider vinegar
1 cup brown sugar
2 cloves
1 teaspoon salt

Makes about 4½ pounds

1

Chop the pears roughly and put them in a bowl. Add the onions, raisins, apple, ginger, walnuts and garlic, with the lemon zest and juice. Put the vinegar, sugar, cloves and salt in a saucepan. Gently heat, stirring until the sugar has dissolved, then bring to a boil briefly and pour in the fruit. Cover and let sit overnight.

2

Pour the mixture into a preserving pan and boil gently for 1½ hours, until soft. Spoon into warm, sterilized jars. Seal with melted paraffin and cover with a cellophane top.

Dill Pickles

Dill is easy to grow and is a delightful herb. It goes well with fish and gives a superb flavor to this popular pickle.

INGREDIENTS

6 small cucumbers
2 cups water
4 cups white wine vinegar
½ cup salt
3 bay leaves
3 tablespoons dill seed
2 garlic cloves, slivered

Makes about 10 cups

1

Slice the cucumbers into medium-thick slices. Put the water, vinegar and salt in a saucepan. Bring to a boil, then immediately remove from the heat.

2

Layer the herbs and garlic between slices of cucumber in sterilized preserving jars until the jars are full, then cover with the warm salt and vinegar mixture. When the liquid is cold, close the jars. Leave on a sunny windowsill for at least 1 week before using.

Rhubarb and Ginger-Mint Jam

Ginger and mint are easily grown in the garden, and they are just the thing to boost the flavor of rhubarb jam.

INGREDIENTS

4½ pounds rhubarb
1 cup water
juice of 1 lemon
2-inch piece of fresh ginger, peeled and bruised, plus 2–3 tablespoons fresh ginger, very finely chopped
6 cups sugar
⅔ cup preserved ginger, chopped
mint leaves

Makes about 6 pounds

NOTE

To confirm the setting point, spoon a little of the jam onto a cold saucer. Let sit for 2 minutes. A skin should have formed on the jam that will wrinkle if you push it gently with your finger.

1

Cut the rhubarb into short lengths. Place the rhubarb, water and lemon juice in a preserving pan and bring to a boil. Peel and bruise the fresh ginger and add to the pan. Reduce the heat and simmer, stirring frequently, until the rhubarb is soft.

2

Remove the ginger. Add the sugar and stir until dissolved. Boil for 10–15 minutes, or until setting point is reached. Skim off scum from the surface of the jam, then add the preserved ginger, the chopped fresh ginger and the mint leaves. Pour into sterilized glass jars, seal with melted paraffin and cover with tightly fitting cellophane tops.

Crab Apple Jelly

Crab apple trees are so pretty with their abundant flowers and glowing red fruit, and though their role in the garden is mainly decorative, this jelly is a delicious way to make use of the fruit.

INGREDIENTS

2¼ pounds crab apples
3 cloves
water (see method)
granulated sugar (see method)

**Makes about 2¼ pounds from each
2½ cups liquid**

1

Wash the apples and cut them in half but
do not peel or core. Place the apples and
cloves in a large saucepan and pour in water
to cover. Bring to a boil, reduce the heat
and simmer until the apples are soft.

2

Strain the mixture through cheesecloth
or a jelly bag into a bowl. Put the sugar
in a heatproof bowl in the oven for
15 minutes. Measure the juice and add
2 cups sugar for each 2 cups of juice.
Pour into a pan and heat gently. Stir until
the sugar dissolves, then boil rapidly until
the setting point is reached. Pour into
warm, sterilized jars and seal.

Rose Hip and Apple Jelly

*This recipe uses windfall apples and rose hips gathered from the rose garden.
The jelly is rich in vitamin C as well as full of flavor.*

INGREDIENTS

*2¼ pounds windfall apples, peeled,
trimmed and quartered*
1 pound firm, ripe rose hips
1¼ cups boiling water
granulated sugar (see method)

**Makes about 2¼ pounds from each
2½ cups liquid**

1

Place the quartered apples in a preserving
pan with just enough water to cover them.
Bring to a boil and cook until the apples
are pulpy. Meanwhile, chop the rose hips
coarsely in a food processor. Add the
rose hips to the cooked apples with the
boiling water. Leave to simmer for
10 minutes, then remove from the heat
and allow to stand for 10 minutes more.
Pour the mixture into a thick jelly
bag suspended over a bowl and leave
to strain overnight.

2

Preheat the oven to 250°F. Measure the
juice and allow 1¾ cups sugar for each
2½ cups of liquid. Warm the sugar in the
oven. Pour the juice into a pan and bring
to a boil, stir in the warmed sugar until it
has dissolved completely, then let boil
until a setting point is reached. Finally,
pour the jelly into warm, sterilized jars
and seal securely.

INDEX

apples: apple mint and pink grapefruit
    fool, 75
  carrot, apple and orange coleslaw, 28
  crab apple jelly, 94
  French apple tart, 78
  rose hip and apple jelly, 94

bacon and cheese quiche, 36
baking, 82–8
beans, beef casserole with, 65
beef: beef casserole with beans, 65
  country meat loaf, 59
  meat stock, 8
  steak and kidney pie, with mustard and
    bay gravy, 64
  Sunday best beef Wellington, 60
  traditional beef stew and dumplings, 62
borage, mint and lemon balm sorbet, 76
bread: harvest loaf, 86
  Irish soda bread, 88
  potato bread, 88
Brussels sprouts with chestnuts, 30

cabbage, braised red, 22
carrots: carrot, apple and orange coleslaw, 28
  glazed carrots with cider, 28
cauliflower with cheese sauce, 40
cheese: cauliflower with cheese sauce, 40
  cheese and bacon quiche, 36
  eggs baked in ham and potato hash, 37
chestnuts, Brussels sprouts with, 30
chicken: chicken and corn stew, 68
  chicken with sloe gin and juniper, 70
  stock, 9
  traditional chicken pot pie, 66
chunky seafood stew, 43
chutney, windfall pear, 91
cider, glazed carrots with, 28
cobbler, rhubarb, 80
cod: cod, basil and tomato with a potato
    thatch, 44
  cod with lentils and leeks, 45
coleslaw: carrot, apple and orange, 28
corn: chicken and corn stew, 68
country meat loaf, 59
country pancakes, 84
country-style pâté with leeks, 18
country vegetable soup, 12
crab: baked stuffed crab, 50
  crab cakes, 50
crab apple jelly, 94
cranberry muffins, 84
cucumber: dill pickles, 92

desserts, 74–80
dill pickles, 92
duck stew with olives, 71
dumplings, traditional beef stew and, 62

eggs, 34–41
  cheese and bacon quiche, 36
  egg-stuffed tomatoes, 38
  eggs baked in ham and potato hash, 37
  eggs in pepper nests, 35
  omelet with herbs, 38
  poached eggs with spinach, 41

farmhouse onion soup, 11
fennel, broiled sea bass with, 49
fish and shellfish, 42–50
  cod, basil and tomato with a potato
    thatch, 44
  cod with lentils and leeks, 45

pan-fried garlic sardines, 48
sea bass broiled with fennel, 49
trout with almonds, 46
tuna with garlic, tomatoes and herbs, 46
fool, apple mint and pink grapefruit, 75
French apple tart, 78
fruit: spiced red fruit compote, 80
  summer fruit gâteau with heartsease, 76
fruitcake, dark, 83

garlic: pan-fried garlic sardines, 48
  stuffed garlic mushrooms, 16

gâteau, summer fruit with heartsease, 76
grapefruit: apple mint and pink grapefruit
    fool, 75
gravy, mustard and bay, 64

ham and potato hash, eggs baked in, 37
harvest loaf, 86

Irish soda bread, 88

jam, rhubarb and ginger-mint, 93
jelly: crab apple, 94
  rose hip and apple, 94

kidneys: steak and kidney pie, 64

lamb: lamb pie with pear, ginger and mint
    sauce, 58
  lamb stew with vegetables, 54
  roast leg of lamb with wild mushroom
    stuffing, 56
leeks: cod with lentils and leeks, 45
  country-style pâté with leeks, 18
  leek and onion tart, 31
  leeks in egg and lemon sauce, 21
lentils, cod with leeks and, 45
lima beans: beef casserole with beans

meat and poultry, 52–72
meat loaf, country, 59

meat stock, 8
muffins, cranberry, 84
mushrooms: mushroom salad with
    prosciutto, 16
  roast leg of lamb with wild mushroom
    stuffing, 56
  roast turkey with mushroom stuffing, 72
  stuffed garlic mushrooms, 16
  Sunday best beef Wellington, 60
mustard and bay gravy, 64

olives, duck stew with, 71

omelet with herbs, 38
onions: farmhouse onion soup, 11
  leek and onion tart, 31
  stuffed parsleyed onions, 33

pancakes, country, 84
pâté, country-style with leeks, 18
pears: lamb pie with pear, ginger and mint
    sauce, 58
  windfall pear chutney, 91
pepper nests, eggs in, 35
pickles, dill, 92
pies: lamb pie with pear, ginger and mint
    sauce, 58
  pork sausage and puff pastry strudel, 53
  steak and kidney pie, with mustard and
    bay gravy, 64
  Sunday best beef Wellington, 60
  traditional chicken pot pie, 66
pork: country meat loaf, 59
  country-style pâté with leeks, 18
  pork sausage and puff pastry strudel, 53
potatoes: cod, basil and tomato with a
    potato thatch, 44
  eggs baked in ham and potato hash, 37
  potato bread, 88
  rosemary roast potatoes, 24
  spicy fried potatoes, 26
poultry and meat, 52–72
preserves, 90–4

prosciutto, mushroom salad with, 16
pumpkin soup, 14

quiche, cheese and bacon, 36

red cabbage, braised, 22
rhubarb: rhubarb and ginger-mint jam, 9
  rhubarb cobbler, 80
rice: stuffed parsleyed onions, 33
rose hip and apple jelly, 94
rosemary roast potatoes, 24

salads: carrot, apple and orange coleslaw, 2
  mushroom salad with prosciutto, 16
  salsify and spinach casserole, 23
sardines, pan-fried garlic, 48
sausages: pork sausage and puff pastry
    strudel, 53
sea bass broiled with fennel, 49
shellfish and fish, 42–50
  chunky seafood stew, 43
soda bread, Irish, 88
sorbet: borage, mint and lemon balm, 76
soups, 10–14
  country vegetable, 12
  farmhouse onion, 11
  pumpkin, 14
  summer tomato, 14
spiced red fruit compote, 80
spinach: poached eggs with spinach, 41
  salsify and spinach casserole, 23
squash à la Grecque, 32
starters, 16–18
steak and kidney pie, with mustard and b
    gravy, 64
stews: beef casserole with beans, 65
  chicken and corn stew, 68
  chunky seafood stew, 43
  duck stew with olives, 71
  lamb stew with vegetables, 54
  traditional beef stew and dumplings, 62
stock: chicken, 9
  meat, 8
  vegetable, 9
summer fruit gâteau with heartsease, 76
summer tomato soup, 14

tarts: French apple tart, 78
  leek and onion tart, 31
tomatoes: baked zucchini in tomato
    sauce, 24
  cod, basil and tomato with a potato
    thatch, 44
  egg-stuffed tomatoes, 38
  summer tomato soup, 14
  tuna with garlic, tomatoes and herbs, 4(
traditional beef stew and dumplings, 62
traditional chicken pot pie, 66
trout with almonds, 46
tuna with garlic, tomatoes and herbs, 46
turkey: roast turkey with mushroom
    stuffing, 72
turnip greens with Parmesan and garlic,

vegetables, 20–33
  country vegetable soup, 12
  lamb stew with vegetables, 54
  stock, 9

windfall pear chutney, 91

zucchini, baked in tomato sauce, 24